W9-CSQ-304

# Easter

Jessica Morrison

Weigl

Published by Weigl Educational Publishers Limited
6325 10th Street SE
Calgary, Alberta
T2H 2Z9

www.weigl.com
Copyright ©2011 WEIGL PUBLISHERS LIMITED

Library and Archives Canada Cataloguing in Publication data availble upon request.
Fax 403-233-7769 for the attention of the Publishing Records department.

ISBN: 978-1-55388-610-5 (hard cover)
ISBN: 978-1-55388-611-2 (soft cover)

Printed in the United States of America in North Mankato, Minnesota
1 2 3 4 5 6 7 8 9 0  14 13 12 11 10

062010
WEP230610

**Editor:** Josh Skapin
**Design:** Terry Paulhus

Weigl acknowledges Getty Images as its primary image supplier for this title.
Every reasonable effort has been made to trace ownership and to obtain permission to reprint copyright material.
The publishers would be pleased to have any errors or omissions brought to their attention so that they may be
corrected in subsequent printings.

We gratefully acknowledge the financial support of the Government of Canada through the Canada Book Fund for our
publishing activities.

# Contents

# What is Easter?

Easter is a celebration of springtime and new life. For Christians, Easter is an important religious holiday. It is a time to celebrate when Jesus Christ rose from the dead. Christians believe Jesus is the Son of God.

# Changing Dates

The date of Easter is different from year to year. It is celebrated on the Sunday after the first full moon in spring. Easter takes place between March 22 and April 25.

# Easter History

For Christians, Easter celebrates when Jesus Christ rose from the dead almost 2,000 years ago. To Christians, Jesus was a great religious teacher. He travelled across the Middle East preaching and performing miracles. Jesus' words attracted many followers.

# The Easter Story

One Sunday, Jesus went to Jerusalem. Many people came to hear him speak. However, he was arrested. The next Thursday, Jesus was found guilty of speaking against tradition. On Friday, he was nailed to a wooden cross and died before the sunset. Jesus' body was placed in a **tomb**. A huge stone was rolled in front of the tomb. On Sunday, three women saw the stone had been moved, and the body was gone. Jesus had risen from the dead.

# The Easter Season

The Easter season begins 40 days before Easter Sunday. These 40 days are called Lent. During Lent, many people stop eating their favourite foods as a sign of devotion. The last week of Lent is called Holy Week. It marks the last week of Jesus' life. Holy Week begins on Palm Sunday. This marks the day that Jesus rode into Jerusalem. Crowds of people welcomed him by waving **palm tree** branches in the air.

# Good Friday

Holy Week nears its end with Good Friday. This is the Friday before Easter Sunday. Christians believe Good Friday is the day Jesus Christ died. In Canada, Good Friday is a holiday. Most people have the day off work and school. Some people spend Good Friday preparing for Easter. This may include painting eggs.

# Past Celebrations

In the 1800s and early 1900s, attending church was the most important part of Easter Sunday celebrations. Women often wore a fancy hat called an Easter **bonnet** to church. At church, people sang hymns. Afterward, church bells rang out in celebration. Family and friends would gather for an Easter meal. They ate foods such as roasted lamb or smoked ham. Many children received gifts. They also took part in Easter egg hunts and egg-rolling contests.

# The Easter Bunny

The Easter Bunny is a large rabbit that hides eggs for children to find. German settlers brought the idea of the Easter Bunny to North America in the 1700s. Today, many children look forward to a visit from the Easter Bunny. Early on Easter morning, children race around their homes and yards looking for hidden eggs and chocolate treats left by the Easter Bunny. Many Canadian cities and towns host large community Easter egg hunts.

# Special Traditions

Canada has many cultures. Often, these cultures have their own Easter traditions. Ukrainian Canadians display special eggs called pysanka in their homes at Easter. Pysanka are decorated with many colours and designs. Ukrainian Canadians also bake a bread known as paska. On Holy Saturday or Easter Sunday, they place paska and other foods in a basket. They bring the basket to church to be blessed. After church, they eat the blessed food.

# Easter Symbols

On Easter Sunday, many churches are decorated with Easter lilies. This white flower is often seen as a sign of new life and hope. **Hot cross buns** are baked during the Easter season. These sweet buns are filled with raisins and candied fruit. Their tops are marked with a white frosting cross. The cross is a symbol of the cross on which Jesus died. The week before Easter, many children decorate eggs. Eggs are a sign of new life and the spring season.

# Glossary

| bonnet | hot cross buns |
| palm tree | tomb |

# Index